MY BOOK OF

Interesting Facts

compiled by

LESLIE KREY

P
PARRAGON

OTHER TITLES IN THIS SERIES:

My Book of Spelling
My Book of Tables
My Book of Grammar
My Book of Simple Maths

Published 1997 by Parragon,
Units 13-17, Avonbridge Trading Estate,
Atlantic Road, Avonmouth, Bristol BS11 9QD.

Copyright © 1996 The Book Company International.

ISBN 0-75252-360-0

Design by Robyn Latimer.
Printed in Italy.

P
PARRAGON

Contents

The Universe

Everything in space makes up the universe. There is no end to the universe and it is always changing.

There are billions of stars in the universe which group together and form galaxies. Earth is in a galaxy called the Milky Way.

Not all the light we see in the sky at night are stars, some of them are planets.

Planets are not nearly as far away as stars. They have no light of their own but look a lot like stars because they shine in the light that comes from the sun.

Nine planets and their moons circle the sun to make up our solar system.

The nine planets are: Saturn, Earth, Mercury, Venus, Mars, Jupiter, Uranus, Neptune and Pluto.

Earth takes 365.25 days to circle the sun. This is one earth year. The further the planet is from the sun the longer it takes.

The Moon is Earth's nearest neighbour which is why we are so interested in it.

Scientists are interested in the moon because it has no air.

The air that surrounds earth cuts down the view of scientists who look at the stars through telescopes.

Our World

To make things easy for you we have split the world into different regions.

Get out your atlas and look up the different places as you read about them.

Western Europe

Countries include: Finland, Norway, Sweden, Denmark, Ireland, United Kingdom, Netherlands, Germany, Belgium, Luxembourg, France, Switzerland, Austria Portugal, Italy and Spain.

The northern countries, Norway, Sweden and Denmark are called Scandinavia. Scandinavia and Finland are very cold and have plenty of snow in winter.

The area in Scandinavia inside the Arctic Circle is sometimes called the 'Land of the Midnight Sun' because in midsummer the sun does not set and in winter it is dark 24 hours of the day.

The Swiss, French and Austrian Alps are well know for skiing.

Most Western European countries are members of the European Union. This was set up in 1991 and helps to encourage free trade between these countries.

Italy produces more wine than any other country.

France, Germany and the United Kingdom are three of the main farming countries.

In 1961 the Berlin wall was built dividing Germany into East and West. In 1989 the first section of the wall was pulled down - the scene of much celebration.

The most famous building in Paris would be the Eiffel Tower which was built to celebrate the Paris Exhibition in 1889.

The largest country in Western Europe is Germany.

The longest river is the Rhine, 1320 km.

Eastern Europe

Countries include: Poland, Czech Republic, Slovak Republic, Hungary, Romania, Croatia, Bosnia, Serbia, Bulgaria, Macedonia, Albania and Greece.

The Parthenon, in Athens, built nearly 2500 years ago, is one of the most famous sites in the world.

Communist rule ended in the 1990's. There is still a lot of fighting going on in many regions.

The biggest city is Athens.

The longest river is the River Danube, 2850 km

Russia

Even though the Union of Soviet Socialist Republics (USSR) has now split into different states, Russia is still the largest country in the world. It is almost twice as big as the United States of America.

The Siberian tiger, one of the world's rarest animals, is now protected.

The trans-Siberian railway is the longest train trip in the world.

The St Basil's Cathedral in St Petersburg was built by Ivan the Terrible, the first Tsar of Russia.

The longest river is Lena, 4271 km.

The Middle East

Countries include: Turkey, Cyprus, Syria, Lebanon, Jordan, Iraq, Israel, Iran, Kuwait, Saudi Arabia, Bahrain, Qatar, United Arab Emirates, Oman and Yemen.

A lot of this region is desert but there are large areas around the rivers that have fertile land. Sometimes deserts go years without rain and if a little rain does fall the air is so hot the rain often dries up before it reaches the ground.

Today most of the people in the Middle East are Arabs except in Israel where the population is mainly Jews.

A third of the world's oil is found in the Middle East.

There is a lake called the Dead Sea which lies between the countries of Israel and Jordan. Around the Dead Sea the air feels thick, hot and damp. No plants and animals can live there because it is too salty. There is so much salt in the water that everything floats.

Mecca is a holy city for people who follow Islam. Many people from all over the world come here to worship.

Unfortunately there is still of lot of fighting going on in Lebanon, Israel and her Arab neighbours. There is also unrest between Iran and Iraq.

South Asia

Countries include: Afghanistan, Pakistan, India, Bhutan, Bangladesh and Sri Lanka.

Most people here are farmers and the main crop is rice. The farmers depend on rain which comes between June and October. Rice is grown in flooded paddy fields and planted in rows.

Elephants are used to do work in many parts of South Asia.

Bhutan is only a small country and it only allows around 4000 tourists into the country each year.

The Himalayas are the world's highest mountain range and Mount Everest the highest peak.

One of the world's oldest religions, Hinduism, is followed by most of the people in India. Pakistan and Afghanistan are mostly followers of Islam.

The Taj Mahal, in India, took 18 years to build. It was built by Emperor Shah Jehan as the burial place for his wife and is made of white marble.

The biggest city is Calcutta, India.

The longest river is the Indus, 2896 km.

South East Asia

Countries include: Burma, Vietnam, Laos, Thailand, Cambodia, Malaysia, Singapore, Sumatra, Philippines, Brunei, Sarawak, Borneo, Java, Sulawesi, Indonesia.

There are thousands of islands in South East Asia. The Philippines has over 7,000 tropical islands and Indonesia more than 13,000.

Many of the island people live on boats or wooden houses built on stilts.

For the most part the land is very rich and rice, fruit and spices are grown.

On the mountains the forests produce woods, like teak and mahogany.

South East Asia also produces more rubber than any other area in the world. Rubber comes from the juice (latex) of the rubber tree.

In the Philippines rice is grown in terraces, some of which have been in use for over 3000 years.

Singapore and Brunei are two of the richest countries in the world. Brunei exports huge amounts of oil. No one in Brunei has to pay taxes.

The Sultan of Brunei has a palace of over 1800 rooms which is probably the largest palace in the world.

In Singapore most of the people live in high rise buildings.

The largest flower in the world is found in Sumatra. It is the Rafflesia and smells so bad that it is also called the Stinking Corpse Lily.

The longest river is the Mekong, 4184 km.

East Asia

Countries include: Mongolia, China, Korea, Taiwan and Japan.

More people live in China than in any country in the world. There are over one billion people living there.

China's best known animal is the Giant Panda which is now very rare and has become a protected species.

The Great Wall of China is the biggest structure that man has built. It is 15ft deep and as tall as a house. It stretches for about 2,400 km. The wall was built to keep out the invaders from Mongolia.

Japan has become one of the richest countries in the world. Japan produces more cameras, televisions and radios than in any other country.

The capital of Japan is Tokyo, the largest city in the world.

The longest river is the Yangtze Kiang , 6300 km.

Northern Africa

Countries include: Morocco, Tunisia, Algeria, Libya, Sudan, Western Sahara, Mauritania, Senegal, Ivory Coast, The Gambia, Sierra Leone, Liberia, Ghana, Mali, Burkina Faso, Togo, Benin, Nigeria, Niger, Chad, Egypt, Eritrea, Djibouti, Ethiopia, Somalia.

Huge areas of Northern Africa are desert. The only way of getting around is on camels. The people of the Sahara are mainly Arabs.

In some areas of Africa there are big rainforests which are home to all different kinds of animals.

The River Nile runs through Egypt and many people live along this river.

The pyramids of Egypt were built over 4000 years ago and were built from large stone blocks. They were built as burial places for kings.

The houses in some Nigerian towns are made from mud bricks that are hard baked by the sun.

The largest city is Cairo, Egypt.

The longest river is the Nile, 6670 km.

Central and Southern Africa

Countries include: Central African Republic, Cameroon, Gabon, Congo, Zaire, Rwanda, Burundi, Uganda, Tanzania, Malawi, Zambia, Zimbabwe, Botswana, Angola, Namibia, Swaziland, Kenya, Lesotho, South Africa, Madagascar.

South Africa is known for its gold and diamond mines. Zimbabwe has iron and copper mines. Kenya and Tanzania are best known for the wildlife.

The cheetah is the fastest moving animal on land and the elephant is the biggest.

The African ostrich is the largest bird in the world, and the giraffe is the world's tallest animal.

The Victoria Falls on the river Zambezi is famous all over the world. The noise of these falls is incredible and they can be heard up to 40 kilometres away.

Off the coast of South Africa is the island of Madagascar. There are animals and plants here that are found nowhere else in the world.

The longest river is The Congo, 4667 km.

North America

North America has only three countries: the United States of America, Canada and Mexico.

Canada is the second largest country in the world and the winters are long and cold. Mexico on the other hand is very hot.

The main tourist attractions in the United States are Niagara Falls, Yellowstone Park and the Grand Canyon. Of course you cannot forget Disneyland in Florida. This theme park is visited by millions of people each year.

Cape Canaveral in Florida is where the first manned space shuttle was launched.

Alaska is a state of the United States. Animals such as moose, bears and wolves are found here.

The American bald eagle is one of the country's national symbols.

The largest city is Mexico.

The longest river is the Mississippi, 6019 km.

Central America and the West Indies

Countries include: The Bahamas, Cuba, Haiti, Dominican Republic, Puerto Rico, Trinidad, Tobago, Belize, Guatemala, Honduras, El Salvador, Nicaragua, Costa Rica, Panama, Jamaica.

Central America is made up of great jungles.

Many of the islands that make up the West Indies are formed from the tips of volcanoes that jut out. A large number of the volcanoes on these islands are still active.

There are 3,000 islands in the Bahamas but only 20 have people living on them.

The Panama Canal was opened in 1914. Before its opening the only way of getting from the Atlantic to the Pacific Ocean was by sailing all the way around South America.

Life in the Caribbean is pretty simple. They do not have the luxuries that the modern world have. It is a popular place for tourists with its warm weather.

South America

Countries include: Colombia, Venezuela, Guyana, Ecuador, Peru, Bolivia, Brazil, French Guiana, Surinam, Paraguay, Uruguay, Argentina, Chile, Falkland Islands.

South America has the great mountain range of the Andes, the jungle around the Amazon river, and desert in some parts of Chile.

The Andes is the longest mountain chain in the world. It has some of the highest peaks in the world and is home to the South American Condor which probably has the greatest wingspan of any bird.

The Amazon runs through the centre of Brazil. Even though it is only the second largest river in the world it carries more water than any other river. On either side of the Amazon is the largest tropical rainforest in the world. It has many rare plants and animals which are in danger because the local people are cutting down the forests to clear land for farming.

Argentina has big grasslands where they keep huge herds of cattle.

The main language is Spanish except in Brazil where Portuguese is spoken.

The Falkland Islands are part of the U.K. Argentina would like to claim the islands as its own and there has been fighting between the two countries over this land.

The highest waterfall in the world is "Angel Falls" in Venezuela. Venezuela also has the most oil rigs in South America.

The Southernmost point of South America is called Cape Horn. They say it has some of the worse storms in the world.

South America is the home of the anaconda, the world's largest snake.

Oceania

Oceania includes: Australia, New Zealand, Papua New Guinea and the islands of Miconesia and Melanesia.

The largest country in this region is Australia.

The first people to settle in Australia were the Aborigines.

The interior of Australia is very hot and dry with big desert areas. Australians call this the 'Outback'.

Australia has animals that do not naturally live anywhere else in the world. The two best known are the kangaroo and the koala. The kangaroo has become the symbol of Australia.

Ayers Rock, near Alice Springs, is a sacred landmark to the Aboriginal people.

One of Sydney's best know buildings is the Opera House.

Almost 2000 kms to the east of Australia is New Zealand.

New Zealand is a beautiful mountainous country and is made up of two main islands.

The earliest people to settle in New Zealand were the Maoris.

The North Island still has active volcanoes.

The Kiwi is the symbol of New Zealand. This flightless bird is covered with long feathers and has a long beak. It lives in a burrow and eats insects and worms. It is now an endangered species. Kiwis lay the largest eggs, in relation to its size, of any other bird.

Most of Papua New Guinea is covered by rainforest. There are hundreds of different groups of people all speaking different languages.

The Poles

If you look at the globe you will see that the North and the South Pole are as far apart as they can get and still be on the same globe.

The South Pole is the coldest place on earth and is very windy. All of the land there is covered with very deep snow and ice.

The North Pole is in the middle of the frozen Arctic Ocean. Eskimos and many kinds of animals, polar bears, reindeers and white rabbits, to name just a few, live on the land around the Arctic Ocean.

If you travelled between the Poles, when you were half way you would be at the Equator.

Plants and Animals

Plants and animals come in many different sizes.

Most plants and animals can be seen easily, such as a horse or a palm tree, but we need help with a microscope to see others.

All plants and animals are made up of cells.

The number of cells depends on the size of the plant or animal. For example a horse would have more cells than a mouse.

These cells make the plant or animal look and act the way it does. Each cell does different things.

Animals have muscles, nerves, blood and skin cells.

Plants have leaf, root and flower cells.

Every living thing you can name is made up of one kind of cell.

Plants

There are over 400,000 different kinds of plants. Plants can live almost anywhere in the world but to do so they need three things.

1. Water
2. Sunlight
3. Minerals

There are 6 main types of plants:

1. Trees
2. Ferns
3. Moss
4. Flowers
5. Seaweed
6. Grass

Plants stay rooted in the same place and make their food using the sun.

Many of our plants grow from seeds.

You can tell the age of a tree by looking at the end of it when it has been cut down.

As the wood inside the tree grows, the tree becomes taller.

Each year one new band or ring of wood grows, making the tree trunk wider.

The colour of the new wood is usually a little different in colour from the last year's ring.

If you count these rings at the end of a tree you can learn how many years the tree lived.

There are millions of different kinds of animals and all of these animals depend on plants to survive.

Animals

Animals are divided into two groups.

1. Animals that have vertebrae (backbones)

2. Animals that have no vertebrae

Most of the animals that live on the land have vertebrae but some of the smaller animals such as spiders, flies, worms and snails have no vertebrae.

There are five main groups of animals with vertebrae.

Mammals
Birds
Fish
Amphibians
Reptiles

Mammals

A mammal is a creature whose first food is its mother's milk. There are many different kinds of mammals. Some live on the land, others in the water and there are those that can fly.

Some mammals lay eggs. The Australian echidna is one of these. The mother echidna lays one egg which she carries in her pouch. The mother's body heat helps the egg to hatch.

Other mammals give birth to live animals the same as human beings do. A few of these include the rabbit, horse, elephant, bear and giraffe.

There are thousands of mammals that can fly. A lot of them are nocturnal which means they come out at night. The best known ones are bats.

Whales spend all their time in the water. They are the largest mammals.

Birds

The biggest living bird in the world today is the ostrich. It is so big and heavy, and its wings so short, that it cannot fly. However it can run faster than any other bird.

A mother bird usually only lays as many eggs as can be kept warm with her body, usually four or five eggs. When they hatch she feeds and protects the baby birds and helps them to learn to fly and look after themselves.

Fish

A mother fish lays more eggs than you can count, often more than a million. She does not stay and take care of the baby fish that come from the eggs. After she drops her eggs in the water she swims away and leaves them to fend for themselves. Other fish and frogs eat them and others float to the surface where they are eaten by birds.

Amphibians

These animals can live on the land and also in the water.

Turtles, and seals spend a lot of their time at sea but lay their eggs and hatch their young on land.

Frogs live on the land but hatch their eggs in the water.

Reptiles

Reptiles do not have as many eggs as amphibians but they are bigger. When they hatch they come out fully formed and are ready to fend for themselves but a lot of them are still eaten by other animals.

Fossils

Some of the animals and plants that lived millions of years ago have been preserved in stone.

Their remains have turned into stone and these pieces of stone are called fossils.

We can look at these fossils to see how animals and plants have changed over the years.

Palaeontologists look all over the world for sites to find fossils from which they gain information.

In this way we learned about dinosaurs.

Dinosaurs

About 100 million years ago the earth began to change and with the change a lot of the dinosaurs could not cope and a big number of them died out, much to the relief of the smaller animals which began to multiply very fast.

The word dinosaur means "terrible lizard".

There were many kinds of dinosaurs that lived almost everywhere.

There was the Brontosaurus (thunder lizard) which weighed as much as ten elephants. It ate only plants and never touched meat.

The Pterodactyl flew and the Tyrannosaur was known as King of the Lizard.

Some of the dinosaurs that once ruled the earth were so big and strong they were not afraid of any other living thing.

Today only the bones of some of the dinosaurs are left.

Human Body

Our body is made up of muscles, blood, and bones.

Muscles

Muscles make up 40% of the weight of your body.

Muscles are used to move our body in different directions.

The heart is also a muscle and it is used to pump blood all over our body.

Blood

Blood is made up of red and white cells.
The red ones carry oxygen and the white ones fight diseases and germs in your body.

Blood is carried around the body in arteries, veins and blood vessels.

Bones

It is important to look after your bones. When you stand, your spine should be curving gently not hunched forward. Remember to keep your chin up, chest out and shoulders back and this will help to avoid putting extra stress on your backbone.

The human body has 206 bones, the smallest one being in the ear. All these bones put together is called the human skeleton.

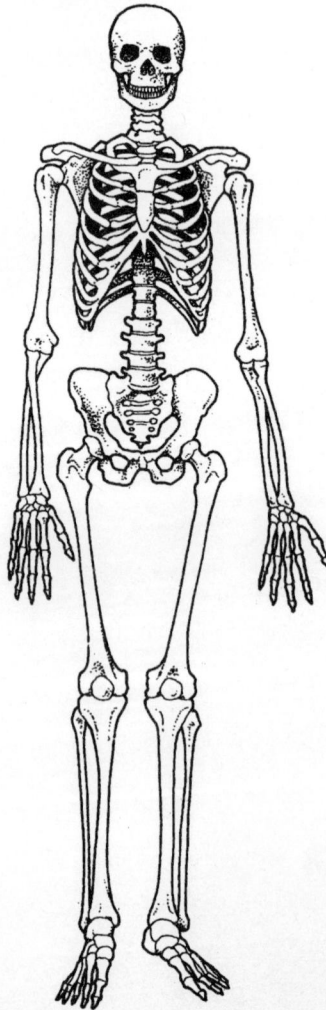

The human skull has 29 bones, 8 of them form the cranium which is the rounded shell that protects the brain.

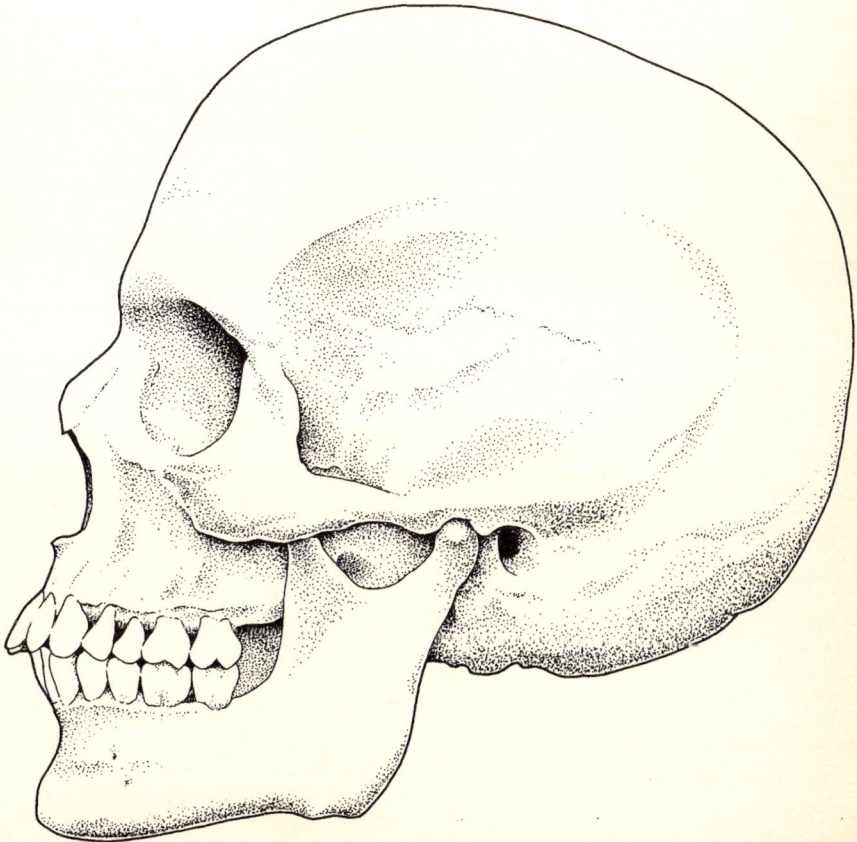

We have 5 senses in our body.

1. Sight
2. Hearing
3. Smell
4. Touch
5. Taste

Sight

Inside your eye, the lens throws light on to a part called the retina. These signals go to the brain then form upside down pictures on the retina. The brain then turns them the right way up.

Hearing

Sound entering the ear makes the eardrum and the tiny bones of the inner ear vibrate. This sends signals to the brain and the brain makes sense of all the noises.

Smell

Millions of cells at the back of your nose can only recognise 15 basic smells. However that is enough for the brain to be able to know the difference between thousands of different smells.

Touch

Nerve endings in your skin feel heat, cold, touch and pain.

Taste

Your tongue is covered with thousands of tiny taste buds. Each bud has a nerve cell that can tell only one taste. It can either be sweet, sour, bitter or salty.

People of Interest

Explorers and Adventurers

Abel Tasman discovered New Zealand in 1642

Captain Cook discovered Australia in 1770.

Robert Peary was the first man to reach the North Pole in 1909.

Two years later in 1911, Ronald Amundsen raced Scott to be the first one to reach the South Pole.

In 1927 a pilot named Charles Lindbergh flew his plane across the Atlantic ocean, the first man to do so.

In 1953 Sir Edmund Hilary and Tenzing Norgay became the first men to climb Mount Everest.

The first man to orbit the earth was a soviet cosmonaut named Yuri Gagarin. His spacecraft took 108 minutes.

The first man to walk in outer space was another Russian called Aleksey Leonov. Actually he did not walk in space he floated.

An American, Neil Armstrong, was the first man to walk on the moon.

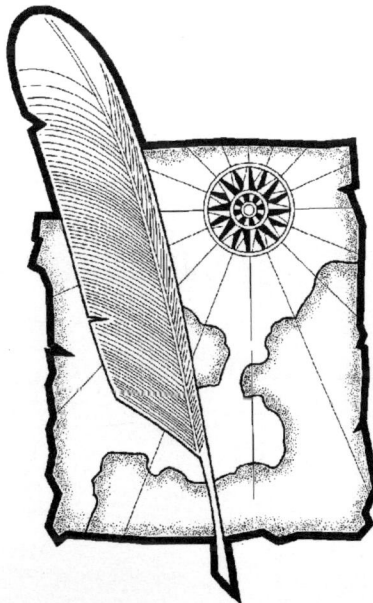

Did You Know ...

In Ancient China it was common practice to clap your hands when you met people.
This was to show that you carried no weapons and meant no harm.
Over the years this turned into our custom of clapping.

?

With just three colours we can make almost all the colours you can see. It takes only yellow, red and blue.

Because yellow, red and blue can be mixed together to make other colours they are called primary colours.

Black and white do not make new colours when they are mixed with other colours. They just make different shades of the same colour.

?

In 1903 two brothers named Orville and Wilbur Wright built the first flying machine in their bicycle shop. It only flew for about twelve seconds before it came down but at last men had learned to fly.

Chalk is a rock that is made underwater.

The chalk we write with today was made hundreds of thousands of years ago. It was made when dinosaurs lived on earth.

At that time the oceans were rising higher and higher until finally they covered most of the earth's land.

In these oceans were many tiny animals. They were so small you could not have seen them. When these animals died their shells fell to the bottom of the ocean and after thousands and thousands of years there were many layers of shells on the ocean floor.

As more and more of the tiny shells pressed together from the top, those on the bottom stuck together.

Millions of years passed after the first chalk was made and the oceans went away from some of the lands leaving chalk layers on the dry land. One of the best examples of this is "The White Cliffs of Dover" in England.

The book that has sold more copies than any other is the Bible.

The first full length coloured cartoon was Snow White and the Seven Dwarfs.

1936 was the year for black and white TV and 1953 for colour.

Leonardo da Vinci painted one of the world's most famous paintings, the Mona Lisa.

Louis Waterman invented the fountain pen in 1884.

In 1939 Germany invaded Poland. Both Britain and France declared war on Germany. In 1941 the Japanese attacked Pearl Harbour and this brought USA into the war.

In 1945 Hitler apparently committed suicide. Germany was overrun.

In the same year an atom bomb dropped on Japan and ended the war.

The seven ancient wonders of the world are:

The Pyramids of Egypt
The Hanging Gardens of Babylon
The Temple of Artemis
The Colossus of Rhodes
Phidia's Statue of Zeus at Olympia
The Mausoleum at Halicarnassus
The Lighthouse on the Island of Pharos at Alexandria.

Over half the earth is covered with water.

?

More than 2000 years ago Homer of Greece and Virgil of Rome wrote great poems and plays that are still read today.

?

In 1928 Mickey Mouse appeared for the first time in the cartoon "Steamboat Willie".

?

One of the most expensive movies ever made was Terminator 2 starring Arnold Schwarzenegger. It cost around US$125 million dollars.

?

Paul McCartney, who was in the band "The Beatles", is the biggest selling songwriter.

?

The biggest selling album is Michael Jackson's "Thriller".

?

Anything that blocks out light makes a shadow.

If you stand in front of a candle or lamp you will see your own shadow. The closer you get to a light the bigger your shadow appears.

In the daytime you have the sun that will produce shadows and at night the moon.

On earth mountains make the biggest shadows.

How could you tell the time if there were no watches in the world?

When the sun is almost directly overhead it is noon. When the sun is halfway to this point it is the middle of the morning and when half way down again it is the middle of the afternoon.

The sun was probably the world's first clock.

People made a sun clock, called a sundial.

When the sun shines on a sundial a piece of metal sticking up from the sundial makes a shadow.

As the sun's place in the sky changes the sun's shadow on the sundial changes.

The first Olympic Games took place in Greece in 776 BC.

The Olympic Games are held every four years, each time in a different country.

A German toy making firm of Steiff claim that they were the first teddy bear maker. Margaret Steiff, confined to a wheel chair, spent many hours making stuffed toys and started selling her stuffed jointed bears in 1902. Her bear was known as "Friend Petz". The Steiff toy company still makes teddy bears today using the original pattern.